An Early Theosophical Controversy

Also from Westphalia Press
westphaliapress.org

The Idea of the Digital University

Masonic Tombstones and Masonic Secrets

Treasures of London

The History of Photography

L'Enfant and the Freemasons

Baronial Bedrooms

Making Trouble for Muslims

Material History and Ritual Objects

Paddle Your Own Canoe

Opportunity and Horatio Alger

Careers in the Face of Challenge

Bookplates of the Kings

Collecting American Presidential Autographs

Freemasonry in Old Buffalo

Original Cables from the Pearl Harbor Attack

Social Satire and the Modern Novel

The Essence of Harvard

The Genius of Freemasonry

A Definitive Commentary on Bookplates

James Martineau and Rebuilding Theology

No Bird Lacks Feathers

Earthworms, Horses, and Living Things

The Man Who Killed President Garfield

Anti-Masonry and the Murder of Morgan

Understanding Art

Homeopathy

Ancient Masonic Mysteries

Collecting Old Books

Masonic Secret Signs and Passwords

The Thomas Starr King Dispute

Earl Warren's Masonic Lodge

Lariats and Lassos

Mr. Garfield of Ohio

The Wisdom of Thomas Starr King

The French Foreign Legion

War in Syria

Nuturism Comes to the United States

New Sources on Women and Freemasonry

Designing, Adapting, Strategizing in Online Education

Policy Diagnosis

Meeting Minutes of Naval Lodge No. 4 F.A.A.M

An Early Theosophical Controversy

C. Jinarajadasa's
The Story of the Mahatma Letters

WESTPHALIA PRESS
An imprint of the Policy Studies Organization

An Early Theosophical Contoversy
C. Jinarajadasa's
The Story of the Mahatma Letters

All Rights Reserved © 2013 by Policy Studies Organization

Westphalia Press
An imprint of Policy Studies Organization
dgutierrezs@ipsonet.org

All rights reserved. No part of this book may be reproduced or transmitted in any form or by any means graphic, electronic, or mechanical, including photocopying, recording, taping, or by any information storage or retrieval system, without the permission in writing from the publisher.

For information:
Westphalia Press
1527 New Hampshire Ave., N.W.
Washington, D.C. 20036

ISBN-13: 978-1935907183
ISBN-10: 1935907182

Updated material and comments on this edition can be found at the Westphalia Press website: westphaliapress.org

Editorial Note:

The early days of the Theosophical movement were marked by controversy, including claims and counter claims occasioned by the so-called Mahatma letters.

Theosophy has gone on to more positive matters, but no student or scholar of the early era can afford to be without these remarks by the one time president of the society.

E

THE STORY OF THE MAHATMA LETTERS

The first letter was received in 1870 and the last in 1900, *nine years after the death of Madame H. P. Blavatsky.*

1. The first letter has inscribed in Russian on the envelope which contains it: "Received at Odessa, November 7, about Lelinka, probably from Tibet. November 11, 1870. Nadejda[1] F." Madame Nadyédja[2] Andréewna Fadéef was the aunt of H. P. B., and Lelinka was the pet name for Helena, the baptismal name of H. P. B. At this time H. P. B. had gone wandering on her travels. The following is what Madame Fadéef wrote to Colonel Olcott in French on June 26, 1884, the translation of which is as follows:

"Two or three years ago I wrote to Mr. Sinnett in reply to one of his letters, and I remember telling him what happened to me about a letter which I received phenomenally, when my niece was on the other side of the world, and because of that nobody knew where she was—which made us deeply anxious. All our researches had ended in nothing. We

---

[1] So in Russian in her signature in pencil on the envelope at bottom left corner, though the letter after "y" or "j" and before "d" is destroyed.

[2] So in the K. H. script in ink on the envelope.

were ready to believe her dead, when—I think it was about the year 1870, or possibly later—I received a letter from him whom I believe you call 'Kouth Humi,' which was brought to me in the most incomprehensible and mysterious manner, in my house by a messenger of Asiatic appearance, *who then disappeared before my very eyes.* This letter, which begged me not to fear anything, and which announced that she was in safety—I have still, but at Odessa. Immediately upon my return I shall send it to you, and I shall be very pleased if it can be of any use to you."

The first letter is on half a sheet of notepaper and is in French, and is now at Adyar. Its script is that of Mahatma K. H. *i.e.* of the letters signed with those initials published in three works mentioned later, and the first of which was received in India in 1880. It has the special characteristic of his script in that *every* " m " has a stroke over it. In a letter to Mr. Sinnett, Mahatma M. referring to H. P. B.'s aunt, asks Mr. Sinnett to :

"Tell her I—the '*Khosyayin*' (her niece's *Khosyayin* she called me as I went to see her thrice) . . ."

(*Mahatma Letters to A. P. Sinnett,* Letter XXXIX). So that evidently the messenger of Asiatic appearance, "*who then disappeared before my very eyes*", was Mahatma M.

2. The next are a series of Mahatma letters received by Colonel Olcott in 1875 in New York. The first of these is "*From the Brotherhood of Luxor, Section the Vth to Henry S. Olcott*". It is signed by three

Mahatmas: Serapis Bey (Ellora Section), Polydorus Isurenus (Section of Solomon) and Robert More (Section of Zoroaster), and at the end of the communication are the words "*By Order of the Grand ∴ Tuitit Bey, Observatory of Luxor, Tuesday Morning, Day of Mars*".

Then followed quickly several letters from the Mahatma who signs "Serapis" to Colonel Olcott. This Adept is often called by Col. Olcott "Maha Sahib". Among these are especially nine letters which are valuable, as they reveal something of the tragic situation in which H. P. B. found herself in 1875 when her work seemed to be collapsing, with no means for her livelihood and no way of establishing herself so that she might fulfil the task given to her, which was to launch the Theosophical Movement. One letter gives a glimpse of this tragic situation in which H.P.B. found herself, which forced her into a nominal second marriage with an Albanian dealer in furs whose culture was about that of a peasant:

" Try to help the poor broken-hearted woman and *success* will crown your noble efforts. Sow healthy grains and choose your soil and the future will reward you by unexpected harvests. Have faith, Brother mine, and when the least expected your eyes may open to such a glorious sight as would dazzle any ordinary mortal. *Try* to help her find the money needed . . . for the 3rd of next month ; give her a chance of showing . . . her noble disinterested generosity and who can tell what may be the result. Her money is certain to return into her hands—it will be easy for you to find that loan for her on such security. O poor, poor Sister ! Chaste and pure Soul—pearl shut inside an outwardly coarse nature. Help her to throw off that appearance of assumed roughness, and any one might well be dazzled by the divine Light concealed under such a bark." (*Letters from the Masters of the Wisdom*, Second Series, Letter 10.)

Another letter refers to the same situation :

" Her cup of bitterness is full, O Brother. The dark, mysterious influence is overshadowing all . . . Tighter and tighter is drawn round them the pitiless circle ; be friendly and merciful to her, brother, . . . and leaving otherwise the weak and silly wretch, whom fate has given her for husband to his desert, . . . pity *him*—also him who, by giving himself up entirely into the power of the Dweller,[1] has merited his fate. His love for her is gone, the sacred flame has died out for want of fuel, he heeded not her warning voice ; he hates *John* and worships the *Dweller* who holds with him communication. At *his* suggestion, finding himself on the brink of bankruptcy, his secret design is to sail for Europe, and leave her unprovided and alone. Unless we help him for the sake of her, our Sister, her life is doomed and for her her future will be poverty and sickness. The laws which govern our Lodge will not allow us to interfere with her fate, by means that might seem supernal. She can get no money but through **him**

---

[1] "**The** dweller on the threshold."—C. J.

she wedded ; her pride must be humbled even before him she hates." (*Letters of the Masters of the Wisdom*, Second Series, Letter 9).

These letters of "Serapis" reveal to us how the Egyptian Brotherhood selected for the starting of the Theosophical Movement three : H. P. Blavatsky, H. S. Olcott and Elbridge Gerry Brown. Mr. Brown was the editor of the *Spiritual Scientist* and the intention was to start from the highest aspects of Spiritualism and broaden out into the facts of Occultism. Mr. Brown, however, drew back from the attempt. Afterwards the Society was started with Col. Olcott, Madame Blavatsky and others.

3. A very brief letter exists, received by Col. Olcott at this period (Letter 24) from the Mahatma called in Theosophical circles the Rishi Agastya, but at the time called by H. P. B. "Narayan", "the Old Gentleman". It is this Mahatma who helped H. P. Blavatsky in the composition of *Isis Unveiled*, often occupying H. P. B.'s body. There is also a second short note from him to Colonel Olcott.

4. Then quite a large number of letters were received by Mr. A. P. Sinnett in India and England and by Mr. A. O. Hume in India, from the Mahatmas K. H. and M., and published in the work *The Mahatma Letters to A. P. Sinnett*, edited by A. Trevor Barker. A memorandum on the publication of these letters, *against* the wishes of the Adepts who wrote them, appears at the end of this monograph.

5. Letters were received by various persons from the Mahatmas K. H. and M., and these appear in the

two volumes under the editorship of C. Jinarâjadâsa, *Letters from the Masters of the Wisdom*, First and Second Series. Explanatory notes have been attached to each letter.

6. Three letters from the Mahatma " Hilarion," one in French, were received by Colonel Olcott in 1883 at Adyar, Madras. The French letter is reproduced photographically as Letter 40, and the first and second transcribed, Letters 43 and 44, Second Series.

7. A letter from the Mahatma called D. K. (Djual Khool) is found in *The Mahatma Letters to A. P. Sinnett,* Letter XXXVII. The script of two of the four pages of the letter is reproduced in the book *Did Madame Blavatsky Forge the Mahatma Letters ?* by C. Jinarâjadâsa, (1934).

Specimen scripts of all the Adept Teachers who have sent communications are given in the book referred to above, and in *The Letters from the Masters of the Wisdom*, Second Series.

8. The last letter received was from the Mahatma K. H. by Dr. Annie Besant in the year 1900 when she was in London. In the *third* edition of my book *Letters from the Masters of the Wisdom*, First Series (1945), I have given the text of the letter with an explanation of how it arrived in London and the situation in the Theosophical Society to which the letter refers. A full size photographic illustration of the letter was given by me in *The Theosophist* for May, 1937. I want to draw special attention to the fact that this letter of 1900 in the K. H. script was received *nine years after the death of Madame Blavatsky,* who was charged in 1885 by the Society for Psychical Research with having forged the K. H. letters.

9. It is on record that a letter completely in the Tamil language, in which neither H. P. B. nor Col. Olcott could possibly write, was received by Mr. G. Muttuswamy Chetty, a Judge of the Small Causes Court of Madras, the father of Mr. G. Soobiah Chetty, who informs me of the fact. There is no trace now of the letter. In Letter 54 (Second Series) from Mahatma M. to S. Ramaswamier appear three words in Telugu script.

Two letters in Marathi were received, precipitated in the Shrine Room at Adyar, and in Col. Olcott's Diary for 1883 are the following entries:

June 4: "In my presence G. V. Joshi received in the silver bowl in the Shrine a note in *Marathi* addressed to him."

December 25: "Grand phenomena at Shrine: 6 or 7 notes to different persons simultaneously appear in the silver bowl—one in Marathi to Tookaram, in which his secret name was written."

"Tookaram" is Tookaram Tatya, the leading Hindu Theosophist of Bombay, on whose letter to Col. Olcott written in Bombay of June 5, 1886, asking for news of Damodar K. Mavlankar, and received at Adyar on June 7, there was found precipitated in transit, Letter 29 (First Series), stating that Damodar had arrived in Tibet. The letter is from Mahatma K. H.

It has been asserted by some who have read *The Mahatma Letters to A. P. Sinnett* that the Mahatmas do not believe in the existence of God, and are in fact atheists. Certainly this view is supported by Letter No. X which begins :

"Neither our philosophy nor ourselves believe in a God, least of all in one whose pronoun necessitates a capital H."

On the other hand there is letter No. LXXVI which says :

"Believe me, good friend, learn what you can under the circumstances—to viz.—the *philosophy* of the phenomena and our doctrines on Cosmogony, inner man, etc. This Subba Row will help you to learn, though his terms—he being an initiated Brahmin and holding the *Brahmanical* esoteric teaching—will be different from those of the 'Arhat Buddhist' terminology. But essentially both are the same—*identical* in fact."

Students of the letters forget that Mahatma K. H. is a Buddhist monk, and that necessarily he and his disciples use Buddhist terminology, as he says above. In the diary of Colonel Olcott of date Wednesday, February 14, 1883, appears the following entry :

"Day before yesterday in Mme. Coulomb's presence there dropped in that room (the Secret room) a note from K. H. and Rs. 150, with a plan of a sanctuary for Buddha and orders to have it constructed."

Now, T. Subba Row, a pupil of Mahatma M., was of equal occult rank to H. P. B. and so greatly did she rely upon his occult knowledge that she placed, in the prospectus of *The Secret Doctrine* issued to the public, the following :

THE SECRET DOCTRINE/*A New Version of* "*Isis Unveiled*"/With a New Arrangement of the Matter, Large and Important Additions, and Copious

Notes and Commentaries./by/H. P. BLAVATSKY/
Corresponding Secretary of the Theosophical Society./
ASSISTED BY/T. SUBBA ROW GARU, B.A., B.L.,
F.T.S.,/*Councillor of the Theosophical Society and Secretary of its Madras Branch./*

T. Subba Row was an Advaita Vedantin of the Shankarâchârya school; therefore, when any philosophical concept related to the Absolute, Parabrahman, the THAT from which the universe comes to manifestation, he was a non-theist, as is any Buddhist. But this did not mean (as it did not mean to Shankarâchârya himself) that, *at the same time*, and from another mode of reaction, he was not theistic. Subba Row, as all Vedantins today, gave his worship and adoration to a Supreme Being, Îshvara, the " Light of the Logos ", as he once phrased it in his brilliant lectures on the *Bhagavad Gîtâ* delivered to the Theosophical Convention of 1886, December 27-30.

Furthermore, if any one presumes that *all* Mahatmas disbelieve in the existence of God, we find the contrary in the following conclusions in several of the " Serapis " letters to H. S. Olcott :

1. " God's blessing upon thee, Brother mine ". (Letter 8)
2. " The great Spirit be with thee, Brother ". (Letter 12)
3. " God's blessing on thee, Brother ". (Letter 13)
4. " God's blessings on you ". (Letter 14)
5. " God's blessing upon thee, Brother mine ". (Letter 15)

6. "God lead thee, Brother mine, and may He crown thy noble efforts with success". (Letter 17)

I quote in its entirety "Serapis" Letter 19, as it reveals the outlook on marriage from the plane of an Adept :

"Know, O Brother mine, that where a truly spiritual love seeks to consolidate itself doubly by a pure, permanent union of the two, in its earthly sense, it commits no sin, no crime in the eyes of the great Ain-Soph, for it is but the divine repetition of the Male and Female Principles—the microcosmal reflection of the first condition of Creation. On such a union angels may well smile ! But they are rare, Brother mine, and can only be created under the wise and loving supervision of the Lodge, in order that the sons and daughters of clay might not be utterly degenerated, and the Divine Love of the Inhabitants of Higher Spheres (Angels) towards the daughters of Adam be repeated. But even such must suffer, before they are rewarded. Man's Atma may remain pure and as highly spiritual while it is united with its material body ; why should not two souls in two bodies remain as pure and uncontaminated notwithstanding the earthly passing union of the latter two.   Serapis."

A little known contribution by Mahatma K. H. appears in a work published in 1883 with the following title page :
THEOSOPHICAL / MISCELLANIES / No. 2 / UNPUBLISHED   WRITINGS / of / ELIPHAS

LEVI./THE PARADOXES OF THE HIGHEST SCIENCE,/*Translated from the French M. S. S. by a*/STUDENT OF OCCULTISM/Calcutta :/Printed and Published/by the Calcutta Central Press Company, Limited/5, Council House Street,/1883.

This work of 115 pages consists of four then unpublished writings of the French mystic and occultist Eliphas Levi as follows :

Preface by the Translator.
1. The Paradoxes of the Highest Science
2. Synthetic Recapitulation.—*Magic—Magism*
3. The Unalterable Principles
4. The Great Secret

The French manuscript was translated by Mr. A. O. Hume who with Mr. Sinnett received certain of the Mahatma Letters signed " K. H." and " M ". This manuscript, intended presumably to be published in *The Theosophist* (though not published in it), had as comments footnotes signed " E. O." (for " Eminent Occultist "). It is on record that these manuscripts were commented upon by Mahatma K. H., for he says :

1. " To reconcile you still more with Eliphas, I will send you a number of his *MSS*.—that have never been published, in a large, clear, beautiful handwriting with my comments all through. Nothing better than that can give you a key to Kabalistic puzzles." (Letter No. XXc.)

2. "*Memo*—At convenience to send A. P. S. those unpublished notes of Eliphas Levi's with annotations by K. H.

"Sent long ago to our 'Jacko' Friend." (Letter No. XXIIIA.). The editor, Mr. Barker, reports: "K. H.'s comments etc. appear in bold type."

3. "In the forthcoming *Theosophist* you will find a note or two appended to Hume's translation of Eliphas Levi's *Preface* in connection with the lost continent." (Letter No. XXIIIB.)

4. "This will perhaps make Eliphas Levi's hints still more clear to you, if you read over what he says, and my remarks on the margin, thereon (see *Theosophist*, October, 1881, Article 'Death') and reflect upon the words used: such as *drones*, etc." (Letter No. XXV).

This article was published in *The Theosophist*, October, 1881, but the footnotes are signed "Ed. Theos.", not "E. O."

The Mahatma in these footnotes of his did not add his usual initials K. H., but instead E. O., which I have been informed were taken by him as on some occasion Mr. Hume referred to him as "an eminent occultist". In the preface to *The Paradoxes of the Highest Science* by the translator (Mr. Hume) appears the following:

"An eminent occultist, E. O., had added a few notes to the MSS. before it reached my hands, and these, which I have reproduced (though some of them will seem scarcely *relevant* to the uninitiated), merit the most careful attention. I too have here and there ventured a few remarks, which must be taken for what they are worth. I do not always agree with E. O., and though perfectly aware that my opinion is as nothing when opposed to his, I did not think it honest to reproduce remarks, which I could not concur in, without recording my dissent."

In many parts of the work footnotes signed E. O., often with caustic remarks on Eliphas Levi, appear interspersed with footnotes by the translator.

The work had been completely forgotten until in 1922 I saw it on the shelves of Bishop Leadbeater's books, and particularly was thrilled—to say the least—by the last footnote by E. O. I had long known with reference to a sentence by Eliphas Levi : " Jesus like all great Hierophants, had a public and a secret doctrine ", that E. O. had said in a brief footnote :

" But he preached it a century before his birth.— E. O."

At my suggestion the Theosophical Publishing Society reprinted *The Paradoxes of the Highest Science* for the sake of the footnotes of Mahatma K. H., and especially for the last footnote, with the message which it gives to the Theosophical Society concerning a work for mankind *which only Theosophists can do.* I have placed a line at the margin of that part of the letter to which I desire to draw the attention of all members of the Theosophical Society.

Eliphas Levi :

" His body fattens the earth and may cause other trees to germinate ; his thought grows in the heavens and will make other thoughts blossom. *For nothing dies, all is transformed, that which no longer is, shall be again, but that*

which was small shall be great, and that which was ill, shall be better."
Footnote by E. O.

"To put it more clearly : we are now well into the second half of the 4th Round, and our 5th Race (*latest subrace of the 4th Race.—Trans.*) has discovered a *fourth* state of matter and a 4th " dimension of space." (?) The 5th Race has to discover before it makes room for the 6th Race, the 5th state and dimension as the 6th and 7th Races have to find out the 6th and 7th dimensions of space and the 6th and 7th states of matter—of *their* planet ; for the men of the 5th, 6th and 7th Rounds (or Astral circuits) will know the states and dimensions of everything in their solar system. Let your exact science, so proud of her achievements and discoveries, remember that the grandest hypotheses—I mean those that have now become *facts* and undeniable *truths*—have all been *guessed*, were the results of spontaneous inspiration (or intuition)—never those of scientific induction. This can scarcely be denied, since the entire history of scientific discovery is there, with hardly one or two exceptions, to prove it. Thus if Copernicus, Galileo, Kepler, Newton, Leibnitz, Crookes (even this latter as may be proved) have one and all *guessed* their grand generalizations instead of arriving at their discovery by long and painful labour, then you have in this a series of truly miraculous acts. The colossal generalizations of the ancients coupled with the paucity of their real data—generalizations that have reached us as incontrovertible axioms—are so many witnesses testifying to the untrustworthiness of our physical senses and modes of induction. The physical Law of Archimedes was not accumulated little by little—it sprung into existence suddenly—so suddenly indeed that the Philosopher who was enjoying his bath at the time, sprung out of it and rushed about the streets of Syracuse like a madman, shouting " *Eureka, Eureka.*" When Sir H. Davy suddenly discovered Sodium by decomposing moistened potash and soda by the help of several voltaic batteries, he is said to have given vent to the most extravagant delight, jumping and hopping about his room on one leg and making faces at all who entered. Newton did not discover the law of Gravitation, that Law discovered him, dropping a visiting card as it were on his nose. Whence these *sudden* inspirations, these sudden rents of the veil of gross matter ?

Occult science not only explains but shows the infallible way of producing such visions of fact and reality. And it shows the means to reach this naturally for future generations. But the authors of the Perfect Way [1] are right : woman must not be looked upon as only an appanage of man, since she was not made for his mere benefit or pleasure any more than he for hers ; but the two must be realized as equal powers though unlike individualities.

Until the age of 7 the skeletons of girls do not differ in any way from those of boys, and the osteologist would be puzzled to discriminate them. Woman's mission is to

---

[1] Anna Bonus Kingsford and Edward Maitland.—C. J.

become the mother of future occultists—of those who will be born without sin. On the elevation of woman the world's redemption and salvation hinge. And not till woman bursts the bonds of her sexual slavery, to which she has ever been subjugated, will the world obtain an inkling of what she really is and of her proper place in the economy of nature. Old India, the India of the Rishis, made the first sounding with her plummet line in this ocean of Truth, but the post Mahabaratean India, with all her profoundity of learning, has neglected and forgotten it.

The light that will come to it and to the world at large, when the latter shall discover and really appreciate the truths that underlie this vast problem of sex, will be like " the light that never shone on sea or land," and has to come to men through the Theosophical Society. That light will lead on and up to the *true spiritual intuition*. Then the world will have a race of Buddhas and Christs, for the world will have discovered that individuals *have it in their own powers* to procreate Buddha-like children or—demons. When that knowledge comes, all dogmatic religions and with these the demons, will die out.—E.O.

"THE MAHATMA LETTERS TO A. P. SINNETT"

The preceding statement concerning *all* the letters of the Mahatmas which have been published, both by Mr. A. Trevor Barker in *The Mahatma Letters to A. P. Sinnett* and by myself in the two volumes *Letters from the Masters of the Wisdom*, First and Second Series, may be useful to General Secretaries of the Theosophical Society for the information of workers from whom questions are asked on the matter.

After the letters had been received from both the Mahatmas M. and K. H., the matter of publishing them was presented to the Mahatma K. H. by Mr. Sinnett in 1884. A reply was received by him in London in the summer of 1884 and is letter LXIII in the book *The Mahatma Letters*. In it appears the following:

"My letters *must not* be published, in the manner you suggest, but on the contrary if you save Djual K. trouble copies of some should be sent to the Literary Committee at Adyar—about which Damodar has written to you—so that with the assistance of S. Y. K. Charya, Djual K., Subba Row and the Secret Committee (from which H. P. B. was purposely excluded by us to avoid new suspicions and calumnies) they might be able to utilise the information for the realization of the object with which the Committee was started, as explained by Damodar in the letter written by him under orders."

In the same letter there appears :

"The letters, in short, were not written for publication or public comment upon them, but for private use, and neither M. nor I will ever give our consent to see them thus handled."

In another letter LV :

"That was *one* of the reasons why, I had hesitated to give my consent to print my private letters and specifically excluded a few of the series from the prohibition."

The same prohibition is referred to in a letter to Mohini M. Chatterjee in a letter of 1884 from the Mahatma K. H.

"You may, if you choose so, or find necessity for it, use in 'Man' or in any other book you may chance to be collaborating for, anything I may have said in relation to our secret doctrines in any of my letters to Messrs. Hume or Sinnett. Those portions that were private have never been allowed by them to be copied by anyone ; and those which are so copied have by the very fact become theosophical property. Besides, copies of my letters—at any rate those that contained my *teachings*—have always been sent by my order to Damodar and Upasika, and some of the portions even used in the *Theosophist*. You are at liberty to even copy them *verbatim* and without quotation marks." (*Letters from the Masters of the Wisdom*, First Series, Letter 39.)

Soon after the letters began to be received in India, certain parts were copied and sent to the workers at Adyar and a few other persons, by instructions from the Teachers, as mentioned above. It is this material that is referred to as being for the "Literary Committee" at Adyar. This teaching omitted all reference to persons, and consisted of extracts from the letters which had the nature of instruction concerning the evolution of man, the planetary system, etc. There was no prohibition regarding any earnest student reading this material. It was largely from this material that Mr. Sinnett in 1883 wrote *Esoteric Buddhism*, a very remarkable work showing his great ability to co-ordinate and systematize into one coherent scheme teachings given in a fragmentary form in the many letters in answer to questions.

In London, when as a boy I stayed with Mr. and Mrs. Sinnett for two years, I well remember seeing on Mr. Sinnett's desk in his library a leather covered box which contained these letters. One night he opened the box when both Bishop Leadbeater and I were present, and showed a few of them, of which I noted especially one of the Mahatma D. K., which is Letter XXXVII, for its unusually neat and small handwriting. Later when I wrote *Did Madame Blavatsky Forge the Mahatma Letters?* and I desired to give a reproduction of the D. K. handwriting, I applied to Mr. Barker and he very kindly had a photograph sent to me of the letter.

Between 1894 and 1895 Mr. Sinnett allowed Dr. Besant to make copies of such of the letters as she wished. She asked her friend Miss Edith Ward to do the copying and copies of a certain number were made and are still at Adyar. During a series of meetings of the E. S., Dr. Besant read from these letters and commented upon them. The number copied was not great and I have no knowledge whether Dr. Besant herself selected them or Miss Ward.

In 1919 I thought it helpful to members to publish such of the letters from the Mahatmas as were with Dr. Besant, and I published the book *Letters from the Masters of the Wisdom*, First Series. It never then occurred to me to use the letters received by Mr. Sinnett, though copies of them were at Adyar. A little time after publishing this first work, Dr. Besant gave me some more letters that had been put away by Colonel Olcott, and in 1925 I published them in the Second Series of *Letters from the Masters of the Wisdom*. A very rich find for this second work were the letters which Col. Olcott had received from the Mahatma "Serapis" in 1875 in New York. They had got mixed up with the old files of the Recording Secretary, and one day the then Recording Secretary, Mr. J. R. Aria, discovered them in a box full of office records and gave them to me. These letters give an utterly new idea of H.P.B.'s work and the difficulties in New York which she had to surmount before the Theosophical Society was started. I cannot help thinking that when Col. Olcott began writing *Old Diary Leaves* in 1895 he must have completely forgotten these letters which he received from the Mahatma "Serapis" or could not find them, as otherwise he would not have given the erroneous view which he does concerning H. P. B.'s second marriage. In the "Serapis" letters one gets a clue to H. P. B.'s tragic self-sacrifice in marrying an Albanian peasant whom she despised and hated. These "Serapis" letters are published in the Second Series as letters 9-17.

I should like to say that in publishing these letters I have carefully kept in mind the possible repercussion of statements in them on the descendents of the recipients to whom references are made, if the references are somewhat damaging to the individuals commented upon by the Mahatmas. In addition, where matters were of a strictly confidential nature between the Adept and the recipient, I have exercised my discretion in omitting such references, as I do not think it right that events that would give rise to discussion today, based on a partial understanding of the events of long ago referred to, would serve any purpose in helping the work of the Society, or make the esoteric philosophy clearer.

In 1923 it occurred to me to publish the material which had been collected by the Literary Committee at Adyar referred to by the Mahatma K. H. During Bishop Leadbeater's stay at Adyar from the end of 1884 to 1886 he had made a copy in his neat, fine handwriting in a large bound notebook. When I saw it as a boy in Ceylon, many of the pages had been affected by damp, and words here and there were almost undecipherable. After the printer began setting up the typescript of this material, to which I gave the title *The Early Teachings of the*

Masters, Miss Francesca Arundale, who knew of the work I was doing, gave me two other copies of the same material, but transcribed in London, from copies sent by Mr. Sinnett. I could supervise only a part of the book through the press, as I was leaving for Europe before the printing could be completed. When putting the material together in book form I sorted it out into sections under topics so far as seemed possible, as Mr. Barker has tried to do with *The Mahatma Letters*.

About this time in 1923, when I published at Adyar *The Early Teachings of the Masters*, Mr. A. Trevor Barker published in London *The Mahatma Letters to A. P. Sinnett*, which of course contained the material in my book. Neither of us knew what the other was doing. On reading *The Mahatma Letters* a year or two after publication, I saw at once that there were many errors in their transcription, and I could correct these from the copies of the letters sent to the Adyar Committee and to London. Early this year I collected together such of the errors as I had noted, and sent a list of them to Mr. T. C. Humphreys, one of the two executors under the will of Mr. Barker.

I should mention how *The Mahatma Letters* ever came to be published. A close friend of Mr. Sinnett during his later years was Miss Maud Hoffman. During his last illness she tended him with the devotion of a daughter. As Mrs. Sinnett had died and the only son, Denny Sinnett, had died also, it was only natural that Mr. Sinnett should make Miss Hoffman his sole legatee.

Once Mr. Sinnett promised Dr. Besant that the letters would be left to her at his death, but after differences had arisen between them on matters of Theosophical administration, evidently Mr. Sinnett changed his mind. Mr. E. L. Gardner informs me : " During his (A. P. Sinnett) last years I used to look in occasionally for an hour with him, and one evening he showed me the whole of the LETTERS that he had carefully filed in three drawers. They would, said he, probably go to Adyar eventually—but he neither said then nor later that such a course had been arranged. As a matter of fact, he was still resentful that his own later writings were not acceptable ! " When Miss Hoffman decided on making the letters public she chose Mr. A. Trevor Barker as editor. Mr. Barker was once a member of the Parent Theosophical Society at Adyar, and Mr. and Mrs. Barker lived a year at Adyar helping in the work. Later Mr. Barker left the Parent Society and joined the Point Loma Theosophical Society then under the headship of Dr. G. de Purucker. Though Mr. Barker knew of the prohibition of the Mahatma K. H. which I have quoted concerning the publication in full of the correspondence, he published all the letters nevertheless.

Had the letters been given to Dr. Besant as was originally planned, whatever parts of them that Dr. Besant decided upon to publish would have been done with an efficiency not possible for Mr. Barker. The letters in his book are not in the right order, and it is only at Adyar, where are the diaries of Col. Olcott from day to day, mentioning events and places where H. P. B. and he visited, that the material exists to find the true sequence of the letters. This work was done by Miss Mary K. Neff whom Dr. Besant put in charge of the Society's archives at Adyar. After many months of study, Miss Neff made out the correct order of the letters and sent a list to Mr. Barker. He, however, replied that *The Mahatma Letters* had been stereotyped and were already in the form of plates and that it was not possible to recast the whole work and put the letters in the order that they were received. Miss Neff published in 1940 a pamphlet at the Theosophical Press of the American Theosophical Society, Wheaton, Illinois, U.S.A. giving the correct order of the letters. A second pamphlet of hers gives the correct order for the book *The Letters of H. P. Blavatsky to A. P. Sinnett.* A second Index to the letters appeared in U. S. A. " Combined Chronology for use with *The Mahatma Letters to A. P. Sinnett* and *The Letters of H. P. Blavatsky to A. P. Sinnett,* arranged by Margaret Conger. 19 pages, Washington D. C., 1939 ".

I close with the copy of a letter to me from Mr. Sinnett on this same topic of publishing in full the letters received by him from the Adept Teachers.

A. P. SINNETT TO C. JINARAJADASA

14, Westbourne Terrace Road, W.
December 14th, 1905.

C. Jinarajadasa Esq.
My dear Raja,

In answer to your specific inquiry, or rather to the one you pass on—for I suspect you yourself will have divined my answer—I should certainly be *not* willing to take any steps which should call renewed attention to any other letters from the Master except those published in "The Occult World." No others ought ever to have been published. It was contrary to His wish and mine that this unfortunate result ensued. The correspondence as a whole was terribly contaminated by what one can only treat as Madame Blavatsky's mediumship in the matter, and a great deal of that which has been allowed to get into print by the distinct breach of faith on the part of certain persons to whom I once entrusted copies, the harder it may be to get at them now the better I shall be pleased. The extracts I published in "The Occult World" were selected with great care, and they, I feel sure, reflected the Master's thought with sufficient accuracy. But it must always be remembered that correspondence from a Master, precipitated through the mediumship of a chela cannot always be regarded as His ipsissima verba. In the beginning of the "Secret Doctrine" some passages are quoted as from a letter by the Master, which I know to be deplorable distortions.[1]

I do not actually wish this letter to be published, but you need not make any secret of what I say in conversation with others.

Ever yours,
A. P. SINNETT

---

[1] See on this charge of Mr. Sinnett against H. P. B., his autography referring to the matter—the famous controversy as to Mars and Mercury—in *The Theosophist*, November, 1946.

At the death of Mr. A. Trevor Barker, the letters were left to Mr. T. C. Humphreys and Mrs. E. Benjamin as trustees. The letters have been deposited by them in the British Museum, the principal library of Britain which is the custodian of many historical documents.

Addendum

It has been stated that several letters in the M. script were received in New York by the late W. Q. Judge. If they have been preserved they must be with the head of the Theosophical Society, once at Point Loma, now at Covina, California. So far as I am aware they have not been published.

Adyar, Madras, November, 1946.

I desire to express my thanks to Mr. T. C. Humphreys for the permission given to quote from *The Mahatma Letters to A. P. Sinnett*.

www.ingramcontent.com/pod-product-compliance
Lightning Source LLC
Chambersburg PA
CBHW061315040426
42444CB00010B/2660